A New Family

Written by: **Shirley Alarie**

Illustrated by: **Ileana Nadel**

Based on real characters and situations at RVR Horse Rescue

for Dominick

Copyright 2016 Shirley Alarie
All rights reserved

Dedicated to
families who adopt rescue animals

Huge thanks to a special team:

Shawn Jayroe, your amazing work has led so many animals to loving, adoptive families. Thank you for your tireless effort.

Ileana Nadel, thank you for your beautiful illustrations.

To my wonderful supporters for this project: Shawn Jayroe, Fran Alarie, Cindy Race, Lexie Jones, Amanda Williams, and Debbie McCoy

The Williams family. You help make RVR Horse Rescue the wonderful place that it is.

Fran Alarie, thank you for believing in me. This Dominick Series is for you!

DOMINICK the donkey and his best buddy, Charity the horse, were as happy as two peas in a pod. Their home at RVR Horse Rescue was filled with loving people and many other animals.

Dominick and Charity spent their days munching on hay and trotting in the pasture. Sometimes neighbors would stop at the fence to pet their noses.

Their days of being abused by bad humans was becoming just a memory. They had learned to trust and love people again, and Dominick thought that life couldn't be more perfect.

One day a man drove an empty trailer onto the property. Dominick knew by now that an empty trailer meant one of the rescued animals was going to their new home. He watched the truck driver walk into their pasture, heading straight for Charity. Dominick was confused and very nervous.

"Come on, Charity," the man said gently.

"Where are you going?" Dominick's voice trembled as he turned to his best friend. Normally they went everywhere together. Why was Charity leaving without him?

Charity looked back and forth between her new owner and her little buddy.

"I'm **sooooooo** sorry, Dominick," Charity said. "My new family is here to pick me up. I'm going to live in a new pasture."

"Oh, no you don't!"

Dominick cried, and big donkey tears streamed down his face.

The best buddies gave each other one last whinny and a quick nuzzle, and then the man led Charity to the trailer and closed her safely inside.

Lucky Charity had a new home with a special family, but it meant leaving poor Dominick behind.

Dominick wanted to be happy for Charity, but he was very sad. He didn't know how he could survive without his best friend.

The nice humans at the ranch gave him extra love and attention, but it just wasn't the same without Charity.

A new family of donkeys arrived at the ranch. Rosita, the mom, Jack-Jack, the dad, and Christian, their baby, welcomed Dominick into their herd.

It was nice to feel like he belonged again, but his new donkey friends just couldn't fill the hole in his heart since Charity left.

Dominick remembered all the good times he had with Charity.

They played chase in the pasture, went on walks around the property, and stomped in the pond.

He missed the cozy, peaceful feeling they had when they snuggled up together in the stall they shared.

The memory of Charity welcoming him when he first arrived at RVR brought him a big donkey smile. Dominick had been so scared. His new friend, Charity, assured him everything would be okay and she had been right.

Before long, the good memories began to bring Dominick some happiness, but he still missed his best friend.

Besides his new donkey friends, Dominick found new horse friends, too.

Big Cowboy and spotted Henry shared his pasture, and they hung out at the hay box together. Dominick started sniffing and nuzzling at old Dusty and his pal, Misty, through the gate that separated their enclosures.

Several barn cats roamed the ranch. Tom had been there the longest and had learned to trust the humans, but Goggles and Turtle were newer. They were both still skittish.

And then there was silly Hormel, the pot-bellied pig. He was a funny fellow. He flopped into his tub of water and then rolled in the mud.

But even with all the other animals around him, Dominick still missed his Charity.

One of the humans began spending extra time with Dominick and he started to look forward to her visits.

He knew he would get a carrot from her back pocket after she brushed him and rubbed his head and kissed his nose.

Before long, his ears would perk when he saw the pretty lady coming. She would give a giant smile and a happy wave as she shouted to him across the pasture. "Hi Dom!"

With her greeting, Dominick would rush to the fence to meet her. He started to get that warm fuzzy feeling of a very special friendship, and suddenly he wasn't as sad about Charity leaving anymore.

One day his lady arrived with two girls at her side. "These are my daughters," she told Dominick.

The girls were just as lovely and sweet as their mom. This time, Dominick got triple the love! All of them showered him with hugs and rubs and Dominick's heart melted.

When it was time for them to leave, Dominick wished they could stay longer.

"It's okay. We will be back," they told him, and Dominick couldn't wait.

During another visit, as the girls pampered Dominick, a man led a huge draft horse into the pasture.

"This is my dad and our horse, Thunder," one daughter told Dominick.

Thunder is one lucky horse, thought Dominick.

Maybe someday Dominick would be lucky enough to have a family of his own.

When it was time for their visit to end, Dominick got sad.

"Don't worry, we'll be back soon," the mom assured him.

Every day Dominick stood by the fence, watching and waiting for the humans who made him feel very special.

Whenever they came, he felt like the luckiest donkey in the whole wide world.

One day, the whole family came together to visit Dominick.

After their pats and rubs and hugs, the dad spoke. "Dominick, we're moving," he started to say, and tears immediately sprung to Dominick's eyes.

"Oh, no you don't!"

he neighed. He couldn't bear to lose this family he had grown to love.

He began to snort and buck.

"Dominick! Dominick!" the mom called. "It's okay! We want you to come with us and be a part of our family!"

"REALLY?" Dominick brayed.

His heart filled with so much happiness.

He imagined hanging out with Thunder in a new pasture, and his family joining them for long, lazy sunny afternoons.

He loved the carrots and apples they always brought him, but more than that, he loved their company.

He would finally have a wonderful family of his own.

"Well, Dominick, do you want to join us?" the little girl squealed.

"Oh, YES I do!"

Discussion Points
for Parents and Teachers:

1. Dominick was very sad when his best friend, Charity, moved. Has one of your good friends moved or gone to a different school? How did you get over your sadness?

2. How do you make new friends?

3. Do you have a pet? How do you make him or her feel like a part of your family?

4. The good people at RVR Horse Rescue take care of animals who need help. How could you tell if an animal needs help, and what could you do?

About Charity and Dominick:

Charity was the first rescue horse of RVR Horse Rescue in Riverview, Florida. When Dominick later came to RVR, Charity befriended him, and they remained best buddies. They shared a stall and could always be found near each other in the pasture.

Charity befriended other donkeys, like the family of Rosita, Jack-Jack, and Christian when they arrived at RVR, but Dominick was her most special friend. Even though RVR Horse Rescue is for horses, the donkeys are also welcome, as well as Hormel, the pig, and the barn cats who wander onto the property, like Tom, Goggles, and Turtle.

Sadly, Charity passed away in her old age and Dominick was lonely without her. A family that includes two girls had already adopted a horse named Thunder. After Charity's passing, the family adopted Dominick so the lucky donkey now has a loving family of his own. He and Thunder still reside on the property at RVR.

Dominick's adoptive family – including Thunder

About RVR Horse Rescue:

Shawn and Dominick upon his arrival at RVR

RVR Horse Rescue was founded by Shawn Jayroe and is dedicated to saving and rehabilitating abused and neglected horses (and the occasional donkey). It is run solely by volunteers, including Shawn.

RVR is not a sanctuary, but rather a home for the rescued animals to build their minds, bodies, and souls to allow them to move on and find a forever home through the adoption program.

At RVR, each horse is provided with the care, training, and space they need to recover. Once the horses are healthy again, they are available for adoption to loving homes.

Follow the incredible adventures on Facebook at RVR Horse Rescue. Or visit RVRHorseRescue.org to make a tax deductible donation or purchase RVR logo products that benefit the rescue.

About the Author:

A New Family for Dominick is Part 2 of Shirley Alarie's "Dominick the Donkey" series - an adorable and heartwarming introduction to animal advocacy, based on real life characters and events.

The "Dominick the Donkey" series compliments Shirley Alarie's adult novel, ***A Healing Haven*** – *Saving Horses and Humans at RVR Horse Rescue*, which is the amazing and moving true account of Shawn Jayroe and her incredible team of volunteers at RVR Horse Rescue. ***A Healing Haven*** is one installment of Shirley's *Lemons to Lemonade Series* of inspirational nonfiction, that began with her memoir, *Losing the Girls*. To contact or see more of her work, check out ShirleyAlarie.com. Follow her writing adventures on Facebook at Shirley Alarie.

About the Illustrator:

Cuban-born artist Ileana Nadel comes from a family of fine artists and architects. Ileana's award-winning creations have been exhibited in many public forums and her artwork graces private collections throughout the world.

Ileana has added ***A New Family for Dominick*** to her growing list of illustrated children's books, including *A New Home for Dominick, New York City Rats, An Opossum Dilemma, Can We Be Friends?, A Christmas Chanukah Wish, I Accidentally...,* and *Pollux: The Funniest Pig Ever*.

Dog training and showing are Ileana's other passions. Her exceptional expertise led to several television episodes on both *The Gentle Doctor* and Animal Planet's *Zig & Zag Alpha Dog Challenge*. She now teaches private and group dog obedience and agility classes in Valrico, Florida at her Cool Critters dog training school. Contact Ileana at ileana@tampabay.rr.com.

www.ingramcontent.com/pod-product-compliance
Lightning Source LLC
Chambersburg PA
CBHW041128300426
44113CB00003B/95